Walking Together

Elder Albert D. Marshall and Louise Zimanyi

Illustrated by Emily Kewageshig

annick press

toronto • berkeley

When we walk together in a good way,
we learn to see the world
through two eyes.

We receive the gifts of Mother Earth through stories.

When we walk together in a good way,
things are revealed.

We hear those who are returning
and those who stayed
sing the Lands and Waters awake after a deep rest.

When we walk together
in a good way on Turtle Island,
we learn we are all connected.

We are never alone.
We need each other.
Mawikwayk. Together, we are strong.

When we walk together in a good way,
we learn about the gifts and stories of our family,
of the Lands, and of the Waters.

Those who were here before us—
and those who will be here after us.

When we walk together in a good way,
we learn the languages of the Land.

When we walk together in a good way,
we give back gifts
by taking care of our family.

We leave things where they are.

We take only if there is enough.
We ask before we take
and we listen for the answer.
We share.

We sing the Mother Earth song.
We say thank you.
We'lalin.
Miigwech.

When we walk together in a good way,
we go to what we love,
we go to what we need—
Water, Stick, Rock, Frog.

When we walk together in a good way,
Frog is one of our teachers.

We wait, listen, and watch for Frog
near the ponds—
we breathe in the stillness.

When we walk together in a good way,
things are revealed.

We hear Frog croaking.
We see Frog.
Frog watches us.
We speak Frog.

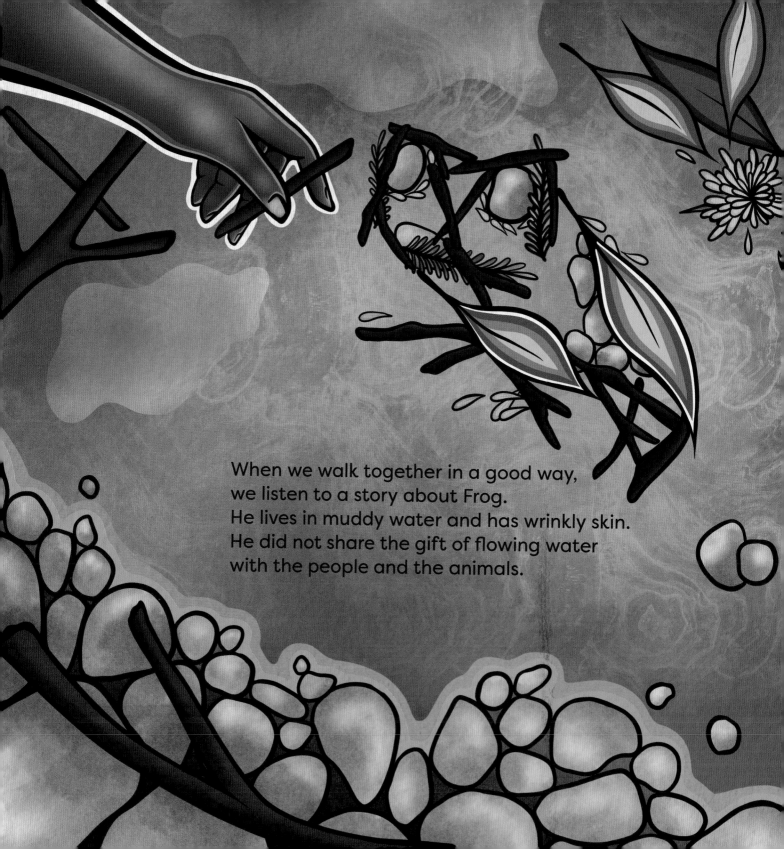

When we walk together in a good way,
we listen to a story about Frog.
He lives in muddy water and has wrinkly skin.
He did not share the gift of flowing water
with the people and the animals.

Ruby-throated Hummingbird, wild Daisies, flowing River, and sunning Turtle are our teachers, too.

When we walk together in a good way,
we share wonder as we wander and play.

Watching stories,
we weave and tell new stories in circle under the Willow.

The stories of the Waters and the Lands
and the teachings of the flyers, the crawlers,
the swimmers, and the four-leggeds
grow inside us.

Like flossy Milkweed seeds,
they are carried on the winds
for future generations.

When we walk together in a good way,
we remember Mawikwayk. Together, we are strong.

When we take care of the Land and Water,
the Land and Water take care of us.

Just like the braided Sweetgrass,
we are stronger together.

When we walk together in a good way,
we learn to know the world
through two eyes.

Afterword

We wrote this story together inspired by the wisdom of the late Mi'kmaq Spiritual Leader and Healer Chief Charles Labrador of Acadia First Nation, Nova Scotia who said, "Go into the forest, you see the Birch, Maple, Pine. Look underground and all those trees are holding hands. We as people must do the same."

In Mi'kmaq, Etuaptmumk means Two-eyed Seeing and Netukulimk means protecting Mother Earth for the ancestors and for present and future generations. Together, these words teach us that when we walk together in a good way, our actions are always in harmony and balance with the Land and All Our Relations. Nature has rights and we have responsibilities. This means we leave Mother Earth a better place than we found it.

Walking Together takes place during Spring, during Squoljuiku's/Frogs Croaking Time Moon. In Unama'ki, Land of the Fog, also known as Cape Breton, Nova Scotia, this is the time when the peepers are active. In Tkaronto—Trees Standing in Water, also known as Toronto, it is the time of flowers blooming and budding leaves, when the Tamarack trees are growing their blue-green needles and the delicate white flowers of the strawberry plants will soon appear.

The Grandmother Moons describe what is happening in nature at that time across Turtle Island: the stories of animal and plant life, the different winds connected to Grandfather Sun, the Thunder Beings, and the Stars in the sky. The stories will be different depending on what Lands you are on.

Everyday, wherever you are, in a park, in your backyard, in the forest, at a river, lake, or ocean, know that you are never alone. Watch, listen, and wonder. What is nature teaching you about the plants and the animals and about yourself? How can you say thank you and show your gratitude?

Share your wonder and curiosity—draw, tell, write, and share your stories. Ask questions, build relationships, and look for different ways to know through your two eyes.

ABOUT THE COLLABORATION

Whenever there is a need for two energies to connect, they will come together. It's the ability of an individual to detect a certain energy that brings peace and openness to get to know this person. We do not question how it was meant to happen. We accept it and honor how we came together. —Elder Albert D. Marshall

A NOTE ON INDIGENOUS LANGUAGES

At this critical juncture, we need to embrace Land as teacher and continue to (re)learn our connection to and with the Land through spirit, heart, mind, and body. During this United Nations Decade of Indigenous Languages (2022–2032) this has to be part of language revitalization as our languages and wisdoms are from the Land.

Mawikwayk: *Together we are strong* in Mi'kmaq
We'lalin: *Thank you* in Mi'kmaq
Miigwech: *Thank you* in Anishinaabemowin

About the Authors and Illustrator

Photo credit: Nadine Lefort

Elder Albert D. Marshall, Honorary Doctor of Letters and Mi'kmaq Spiritual Leader, is from the Moose Clan of the Mi'kmaq Nation. He lives in the community of Eskasoni—*where the fir trees are plenty*—in Unama'ki Land of the Fog (Cape Breton), Nova Scotia, the Traditional Territory of the Mi'kma'ki. He has been working to bring forward the concept of Two-Eyed Seeing—learning to see from one eye with the strengths of (or best in) Indigenous knowledges and ways of knowing, and learning to see from the other eye with the strengths of (or best in) non-Indigenous knowledges and ways of knowing—and most importantly, using both of these eyes together to know your gifts and responsibilities for the benefit of All Our Relations, for Mother Earth.

My favorite moments were to just go and be in the woods, you just get a wonderful feeling. If you could explain happiness, when you are in the forest nothing scares you, you feel so at home. A place of comfort and healing and to restore balance.

Louise Zimanyi, of French-Canadian and Hungarian descent, is a mother, professor, and researcher and lives, works, and plays in Tkaronto—Trees Standing in Water (Toronto), part of Treaty 13 and the Dish with One Spoon territory. She explores how Earth-centered pedagogy and practice in the early years can plant the seeds of sustainability for current and future generations through respectful relationships and reciprocity.

My favorite outdoor play memories when I was young were at the beach: my red bathing suit with white piping, slow play with sand, water, shells, rocks, and sticks, swimming in waves, and picnic lunches.

Emily Kewageshig is an Anishnaabe artist and visual storyteller whose work captures the interconnection of life forms using both traditional and contemporary materials and methods. She creates artwork that highlights Indigenous knowledge and culture. Emily is from Saugeen First Nation in Ontario, Canada.

When I am searching for the feeling of peace and happiness I always return to the forests. My son Lawson and I have enjoyed spending so many of our days hiking, following animal tracks, collecting rocks for our growing collection, and taking in the beautiful Lake Huron sunsets. Nature makes us feel the most alive and always has something new to teach us, and for that we are forever grateful.

Photo credit:
Shelby Andrews Photography

To our past, present, and future knowledge holders.
—Elder Albert D. Marshall

To all who carry, create, tell, and inspire stories through their words
and art . . . the world needs more storytellers and listeners.
—Louise Zimanyi

To Lawson.
—Emily Kewageshig

© 2023 Elder Albert D. Marshall and Louise Zimanyi (text)
© 2023 Emily Kewageshig (illustrations)
First paperback printing (fifth printing) June 2024

Cover art by Emily Kewageshig, designed by Marijke Friesen and Paul Covello
Interior designed by Marijke Friesen and Paul Covello
Edited by Stephanie Strachan and Mary Beth Leatherdale

Annick Press Ltd.

We acknowledge the support of the Canada Council for the Arts and the Ontario Arts Council, and the participation of the Government of Canada/la participation du gouvernement du Canada for our publishing activities.

Library and Archives Canada Cataloguing in Publication

Title: Walking together / Elder Albert Marshall & Louise Zimanyi ; illustrated by Emily Kewageshig.
Names: Marshall, Albert (Albert D.), author. | Zimanyi, Louise, author. | Kewageshig, Emily, illustrator.
Identifiers: Canadiana (print) 20220419868 | Canadiana (ebook) 20220419957 | ISBN 9781773217765 (hardcover) | ISBN 9781773217789 (HTML) | ISBN 9781773217796 (PDF)
Subjects: LCSH: Human ecology—Juvenile literature. | LCSH: Traditional ecological knowledge—Juvenile literature. | CSH: Mi'kmaq—Juvenile literature.
Classification: LCC GF48 .M37 2023 | DDC j304.2—dc23

Library and Archives Canada Cataloguing in Publication

Title: Walking together / Elder Albert D. Marshall and Louise Zimanyi ; illustrated by Emily Kewageshig.
Names: Marshall, Albert (Albert D.), author. | Zimanyi, Louise, author. | Kewageshig, Emily, illustrator.
Description: Previously published: Toronto; Berkeley: Annick Press, 2023.
Identifiers: Canadiana 20240298802 | ISBN 9781773217772 (softcover)
Subjects: LCSH: Human ecology—Juvenile literature. | LCSH: Traditional ecological knowledge—Juvenile literature. | LCSH: Indigenous peoples—Nova Scotia—Juvenile literature. | CSH: Mi'kmaq—Juvenile literature. | LCGFT: Picture books. | LCGFT: Creative nonfiction.
Classification: LCC GF48 .M37 2024 | DDC j304.2—dc23

Published in the U.S.A. by Annick Press (U.S.) Ltd.
Distributed in Canada by University of Toronto Press.
Distributed in the U.S.A. by Publishers Group West.

Printed in China

annickpress.com
emily-kewageshig.com

Also available as an e-book. Please visit annickpress.com/ebooks for more details.